Carol Sowatsky   10/30/03

May these stories renew your soul and strengthen your faith in God.

Thanks for being my forever friend. You are an inspiration to me. I'll always cherish the times God has allowed us to be together to laugh, share and be serious. Thanks for hosting me these 8 days.

"There is a place where spirits blend, where friend holds fellowship with friend, Thou sundered far by faith they meet, Around one common mercy seat." ☺☺

Never stop licking that finger! My kindred spirit, Mary F.

Stories *for a* Cheerful Heart

(*Keepsakes for the Heart* is an elegant gift collection that
includes a hardbound book with full-color artwork,
complementary bookmark, note cards,
and a charming box for keepsakes.)

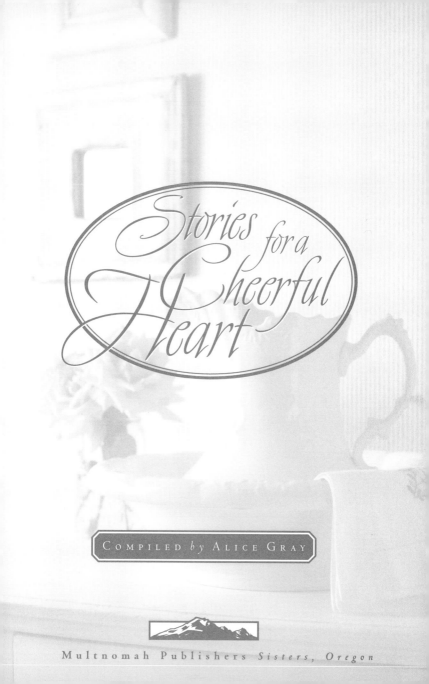

Stories for a Cheerful Heart

COMPILED by ALICE GRAY

Multnomah Publishers *Sisters, Oregon*

STORIES FOR A CHEERFUL HEART
published by Multnomah Publishers, Inc.

© 2000 by Multnomah Publishers, Inc.
International Standard Book Number: 1-57673-683-0

Cover image by PhotoDisc
Cover design by The Office of Bill Chiaravalle

Scripture quotes are taken from
The Holy Bible, King James Version

Multnomah is a trademark of Multnomah Publishers, Inc.,
and is registered in the U.S. Patent and Trademark Office.

The colophon is a trademark of Multnomah Publishers, Inc.

Printed in the United States of America

For information:
MULTNOMAH PUBLISHERS, INC.
POST OFFICE BOX 1720
SISTERS, OREGON 97759

Library of Congress Cataloging-in-Publication Data
Stories for a cheerful heart/[compiled] by Alice Gray.
    p. cm.
    ISBN 1-57673-683-0
    1. Conduct of life—Anecdotes, I. Gray, Alice, 1939-
    BJ1597 .S75 2000
    242—dc21

                             00-009612

00 01 02 03 04 05 06—10 9 8 7 6 5 4 3 2 1 0

CHEERFULNESS

Cheerfulness is a yellow umbrella

covering the rainy days of life.

Kimber Annie Engstrom

CONTENTS

SUNNY MOMENTS

LOVE AND THE CABBIE
Art Buchwald

FROM *STORIES FOR A KINDRED HEART*

I was in New York the other day and rode with a friend in a taxi. When we got out, my friend said to the driver, "Thank you for the ride. You did a superb job of driving."

The taxi driver was stunned for a second. Then he said, "Are you a wise guy or something?"

"No, my dear man, and I'm not putting you on. I admire the way you keep cool in heavy traffic."

"Yeah," the driver said and drove off.

"What was that all about?" I asked.

"I am trying to bring love back to New York," he said. "I believe it's the only thing that can save the city."

"How can one man save New York?"

"It's not one man. I believe I have made that taxi driver's day. Suppose he has twenty fares. He's going to be nice to those twenty fares because someone was nice to him. Those fares in turn will be kinder to their employees or shopkeepers or waiters or even their own families. Eventually the goodwill could spread to at least one

thousand people. Now that isn't bad, is it?"

"But you're depending on that taxi driver to pass your goodwill to others."

"I'm not depending on it," my friend said. "I'm aware that the system isn't foolproof so I might deal with ten different people today. If out of ten I can make three happy, then eventually I can indirectly influence the attitudes of three thousand more."

"It sounds good on paper," I admitted, "but I'm not sure it works in practice."

"Nothing is lost if it doesn't. It didn't take any of my time to tell that man he was doing a good job. He neither received a larger tip nor a smaller tip. If it fell on deaf ears, so what? Tomorrow there will be another taxi driver I can try to make happy."

"You're some kind of a nut," I said.

"That shows how cynical you have become. I have made a study of this. The thing that seems to be lacking, besides money of course, for our postal employees, is that no one tells people who work for the post office what a good job they're doing."

"But they're not doing a good job."

"They're not doing a good job because they feel no one cares if they do or not. Why shouldn't someone say a kind word to them?"

We were walking past a structure in the process of being built

and passed five workmen eating their lunch. My friend stopped. "That's a magnificent job you men have done. It must be difficult and dangerous work."

The workmen eyed my friend suspiciously.

"When will it be finished?"

"June," a man grunted.

"Ah. That really is impressive. You must all be very proud."

We walked away. I said to him, "I haven't seen anyone like you since *The Man from LaMancha.*"

"When those men digest my words, they will feel better for it. Somehow the city will benefit from their happiness."

"But you can't do this all alone!" I protested. "You're just one man."

"The most important thing is not to get discouraged. Making people in the city become kind again is not an easy job, but if I can enlist other people in my campaign..."

"You just winked at a very plain-looking woman," I said.

"Yes, I know," he replied. "And if she's a schoolteacher, her class will be in for a fantastic day."

L E S S O N   I N   F O R G I V E N E S S

Jerry Harpt

orty-five years seems like a long time to remember the name of a mere acquaintance. I have duly forgotten the name of an old lady who was a customer on my paper route when I was a twelve-year-old boy in Marinette, Wisconsin, back in 1954. Yet it seems like just yesterday that she taught me a lesson in forgiveness that I can only hope to pass on to someone else someday.

On a mindless Saturday afternoon, a friend and I were throwing rocks onto the roof of the old lady's house from a secluded spot in her backyard. The object of our play was to observe how the rocks changed to missiles as they rolled to the roof's edge and shot out into the yard like comets falling from the sky.

I found myself a perfectly smooth rock and sent it for a ride. The stone was too smooth, however, so it slipped from my hand as I let it go and headed straight for a small window on the old lady's back porch. At the sound of fractured glass, we took off from the old lady's yard faster than any of our missiles flew off her roof.

I was too scared about getting caught that first night to be concerned about the old lady with the broken porch window. However,

a few days later, when I was sure that I hadn't been discovered, I started to feel guilty for her misfortune. She still greeted me with a smile each day when I gave her the paper, but I was no longer able to act comfortable in her presence.

I made up my mind that I would save my paper delivery money, and in three weeks I had the seven dollars that I calculated would cover the cost of her window. I put the money in an envelope with a note explaining that I was sorry for breaking her window and hoped that the seven dollars would cover the cost for repairing it.

I waited until it was dark, snuck up to the old lady's house, and put the envelope of retribution through the letter slot in her door. My soul felt redeemed, and I couldn't wait for the freedom of, once again, looking straight into the old lady's eyes.

The next day, I handed the old lady her paper and was able to return the warm smile that I was receiving from her. She thanked me for the paper and said, "Here, I have something for you." It was a bag of cookies. I thanked her and proceeded to eat the cookies as I continued my route.

After several cookies, I felt an envelope and pulled it out of the bag. When I opened the envelope, I was stunned. Inside was the seven dollars and a short note that said, "I'm proud of you."

A R E   W E   R I C H ?

Erma Bombeck

F R O M   F O R E V E R ,   E R M A

The other day out of a clear blue sky Brucie asked, "Are we rich?"

I paused on my knees as I retrieved a dime from the sweeper bag, blew the dust off it and asked, "Not so you can notice. Why?"

"How can you tell?" he asked.

I straightened up and thought a bit. Being rich is a relative sort of thing. Here's how I can always tell.

"You're rich when you buy your gas at the same service station all the time so your glasses match.

"You're rich when you can have eight people to dinner and don't have to wash forks between the main course and dessert.

"You're rich when you buy clothes for your kids that are two sizes too big for the one you buy 'em for and four sizes too big for the one that comes after him.

"You're rich when you own a boat—without oars.

"You can tell people have money when they record a check and don't have to subtract it right away.

"People have money when they sit around and joke with the cashier while she's calling in their charge to see if it's still open.

"You're rich when you write notes to the teacher on paper without lines.

"You're rich when your television set has all the knobs on it.

"You're rich when you can throw away a pair of pantyhose just because it has a large hole in it.

"You know people are loaded when they don't have to save rubber bands from the celery and store them on a doorknob.

"You're rich when you can have a home wedding without HAVEN FUNERAL HOME stamped on the folding chairs.

"You're rich when the Scouts have a paper drive and you have a stack of *The New York Times* in your basement.

"You're rich when your dog is wet and smells good.

"You're rich when your own hair looks so great everyone thinks it's a wig."

Brucie sat quietly for a moment, then said, "I think my friend Ronny is rich."

"How can you tell?" I asked.

"His mom buys his birthday cake at a bakery, and it isn't even cracked on top."

"He's rich, all right," I sighed.

WE COULD HAVE
DANCED ALL NIGHT
Guy Rice Doud
FROM *MOLDER OF DREAMS*

As adviser to our high school student council I worked with the leadership to encourage projects that involved student service. I was impressed with my students' enthusiasm for helping with local canned food drives and other events to aid charity.

Our "Adopt-a-grandparent" program had been rewarding for the students who had been involved. They had grown as people by discovering the worth of others. I believe that the true leader is the true servant, and I tried to convey that message to my students. But it never got through to them as clearly as it did the night of the prom.

Tom Rosenberger had given me a call. A friend, and one of the local elementary principals, Tom had heard of an idea at a conference he had attended and called to share the idea with me. I fell in love with it and soon shared it with my student council.

"Mr. President?" I asked.

Mike, the president of the student council, acknowledged me. "Yes, Mr. Doud?"

I started gradually. "I've been thinking of an idea, and I want to bounce it off everyone."

"What's the idea?" asked Mike.

"I think we should host a prom." I said.

"We already have a prom!" answered about thirty students all at once, who seemed to wonder if I had lost my mind. They knew that organizing the prom was the responsibility of the junior class cabinet.

"Oh, I don't mean a prom for eleventh and twelfth graders," I said.

"We're not going to include sophomores!" said one senior boy.

"No. I want to have a prom for senior—" but they didn't let me finish.

"Seniors can already go to the prom," Mike answered, wondering what had gone wrong with his adviser.

"No, for senior citizens. People fifty-five years of age and over. Let's hold a prom for them."

"Why would we want to do that?" asked Mike.

"Let's take the money we've earned this year," I said, "and let's give it back to the community in the form of a gift. That gift will be a prom. We'll invite all senior citizens to come. We'll decorate the gym, hire an orchestra, have corsages for the ladies..." I was

beginning to show some real excitement.

"If we spend money doing that, does that mean we wouldn't take our usual spring trip?" asked one girl, putting down the mirror she held in her hand.

"We would spend as much of the money as necessary to make this a most special evening for the senior citizens. The orchestra we hire will play the big band sounds of the twenties and thirties and other dance music. I've already contacted an orchestra, and I've talked with our principal, who thinks it's a great idea. I told him that I thought you guys would think it's a great idea, too." I can be pretty persuasive sometimes.

After much discussion, the council voted to form a committee to plan the senior citizen prom. In the weeks to follow, I watched my students become excited about the prom. Some of the young men in the council decided to order tuxedos so they would look nice as hosts. The girls planned to wear their long dresses to serve as hostesses.

All of Brainerd got excited the week before the prom. Paul Harvey began page two of his national daily broadcast this way: "In Brainerd, Minnesota, the student council is planning a prom...for senior citizens. That's right! A prom...for senior citizens. The Brainerd students are going to provide an orchestra, corsages, valet

parking, free hors d'oeuvres and...they are also going to do the chaperoning!"

I had been somewhat concerned about the lack of advertising. My students had contacted the senior citizen centers in the area and had sent out invitations, but when I heard it announced by Paul Harvey, my fears of poor publicity died.

The night of the prom finally arrived. The students had decorated our gym more beautifully than I had ever seen it. It was like the gym I had seen in my dreams when I had been in high school. The floral department at the vocational school had donated corsages, some of the local banks provided the hors d'oeuvres, the bus company that contracts with the school district provided free transportation to any senior citizen needing it. My students had tried to cover all the bases. We sat back to wait and see how many seniors would attend. The prom was to begin at six-thirty. At four o'clock, they started to come.

One of the first to arrive was an older lady with a cane. She stopped inside the door and looked around.

"Oh," she said, "so this is the new high school."

I didn't remind her that the high school was more than fifteen years old.

"I've never been in here before," she said.

Mark Dinham, one of the main organizers of the prom, grabbed a corsage and asked her if he could pin it on her. She readily agreed.

"The prom doesn't begin until six-thirty," Mark said.

"I'll wait," she said. "I want to get a good seat."

"I hope you'll do some dancing," I said.

"I'll dance if you dance with me," she replied as Mark finished pinning her corsage.

He turned a bit red. "Sure, I'll dance with you, but I've got to go home and change clothes," he said.

A few moments later, a couple walked up to the table. "Is this where the prom is being held?" they asked.

"That's right," I said.

I could hardly believe what they had to say: "We're from Oregon, and we're on our way to Wisconsin. We heard it on Paul Harvey yesterday, so we looked up Brainerd on the map and decided to go a little out of our way so we could come to your prom. Are we welcome?"

And people kept coming. By six-thirty when the prom began, more than five hundred senior citizens packed the transformed gymnasium. But we had developed one major problem. Mike was the first to call it to my attention. I had noticed him dancing with

one lady after another. He wasn't able to take a break.

"Mr. Doud," he said, "we have a serious male shortage here."

"What are you going to do about it, Mike?" I asked.

"I know where some of the hockey team is tonight, and I think I could call them and tell them to go home and get their suits on and get over here."

"Good plan," I said.

Soon some of Mike's friends started to arrive. I watched as the lady who had been the first to come walked up to one of the sophomores who had just entered the gym.

"You come dance with me," she said, grabbing his hand before he was sure what had happened.

Mike came up to me. "This is fun. Where did they learn to dance like this?"

Mike and many of my students were amazed that some dances actually had set steps and patterns. I joined in as the senior citizens taught me to waltz and polka. I had never learned to dance, either. One of the seniors who had dressed up for the occasion had on a beautiful long dress with sequins, and the mirrored ball in the middle of the dance floor reflected light off her dress. We danced. She led. "If I were about sixty years younger, I'd go after you," she said and laughed.

"What grade are you in?" she asked.

I laughed harder. "I'm a teacher here. I'm in charge of these kids."

"Oh," she said, "You're so young and handsome."

I didn't laugh. "And you are very beautiful," I said.

"Oh, come on now..."

The orchestra began to play a song from *My Fair Lady*, and as I followed my partner, I thought of Eliza Doolittle. Henry Higgins saw an elegant woman when everyone else saw a peasant.

"I could have danced all night..." My partner sang along with the music.

"That was a good movie," she added, "but I bet it's before your time."

"No, I remember it well." I looked about at my students, every one of them dancing with a senior citizen.

One older man was teaching a sophomore girl how to waltz. I watched her. I was used to seeing her in torn blue jeans. She was beautiful in a long dress.

When the evening finally came to an end, no one wanted to leave. Mike walked up to me. "That was the most fun I've ever had in high school."

"You mean that was more fun than your junior-senior proms?" I asked.

"No question about it." Mike was definite.

"What made this so much fun?" I asked.

Without thinking for even a moment, Mike answered, "It really feels good to do something for somebody else."

The following Monday, Paul Harvey, who must have spies all about, concluded his broadcast with this story: "Remember last week I told you about how the Brainerd, Minnesota, student council was going to host a prom for senior citizens? Well, they did and more than five hundred senior citizens showed up.

"The high school students danced with the seniors, and the chaperons reported no major problems.... Oh, there was a little smooching in the corner, but no major problems. Paul Harvey, good day."

When the wings of cheerfulness
Take to flight
The heart is lifted up.
— *K i m b e r   A n n i e   E n g s t r o m*

CALLING LONG DISTANCE

I read about one man who called his wife from an airport pay phone. When he had used up all his coins, the operator interrupted to say he had one minute left. The man hurriedly tried to finish his conversation with his wife, but before they could tell each other good-bye, the line went dead. With a sigh, the man hung up the phone and started to leave the little telephone cubicle. Just then the phone rang. Thinking it was the operator wanting more money, the man almost didn't answer. But something told him to pick up the phone. And sure enough, it was the operator. But she didn't want more money. Instead she had a message for him.

"After you hung up, your wife said she loved you," the operator said. "I thought you'd want to know."

Barbara Johnson

FROM *WE BRAKE FOR JOY!*

T O O T H L E S S   G R I N

Sharon Palmer

was doing some last-minute Christmas shopping in a toy store and decided to look at fashion dolls. A nicely dressed little girl was excitedly looking through the same dolls as well, with a roll of money clamped tightly in her little hand. When she came upon a doll she liked, she would turn and ask her father if she had enough money to buy it. He usually said yes but she would keep looking and keep going through their ritual of "do I have enough?"

As she was looking, a little boy wandered in across the aisle and started sorting through some of the video games. He was dressed neatly, but in clothes that were obviously rather worn, and wearing a jacket that was probably a couple of sizes too small. He, too, had money in his hand, but it looked to be no more than five dollars or so, at the most. He was with his father as well, but each time he picked one of the video games and looked at his father, his father shook his head.

The little girl had apparently chosen her doll, a beautifully dressed, glamorous creation that would have been the envy of every

little girl on the block. However, she had stopped and was watching the interchange between the little boy and his father. Rather dejectedly, the boy had given up on the video games and had chosen what looked like a book of stickers instead. He and his father then started walking through another aisle of the store.

The little girl put her carefully chosen doll back on the shelf, and ran over to the video games. She excitedly picked up one that was lying on top of the other toys, and raced toward the checkout after speaking with her father. I picked up my purchases and got in line behind them. Then, much to the little girl's obvious delight, the little boy and his father got in line behind me.

After the toy was paid for and bagged, the little girl handed it back to the cashier and whispered something in her ear. The cashier smiled and put the package under the counter. I paid for my purchases and was rearranging things in my purse when the little boy came up to the cashier.

The cashier rang up his purchases and then said, "Congratulations, you have been selected to win a prize!" With that, she handed the little boy the video game, and he could only stare in disbelief. It was, he said, exactly what he had wanted!

The little girl and her father had been standing at the doorway

during all of this, and I saw the biggest, prettiest, toothless grin on that little girl that I have ever seen in my life. Then they walked out the door, and I followed, close behind them.

As I walked back to my car, in amazement over what I had just witnessed, I heard the father ask his daughter why she had done that. I'll never forget what she said to him. "Daddy, didn't Nana and PawPaw want me to buy something that would make me happy?" He said, "Of course they did, honey." To which the little girl replied, "Well, I just did!" With that, she giggled and started skipping toward their car.

I had just witnessed the Christmas spirit in that toy store, in the form of a little girl who understands more about the reason for the season than most adults I know! May God bless her and her parents, just as she blessed that little boy, and me, that day!

A   S I N G L E   C R O C U S

Joan Wester Anderson

FROM *WHERE WONDERS PREVAIL*

*I*t was an autumn morning shortly after my husband and I moved into our first house. Our children were upstairs unpacking, and I was looking out the window at my father moving around mysteriously on the front lawn. My parents lived nearby, and Dad had visited us several times already. "What are you doing out there?" I called to him.

He looked up, smiling. "I'm making you a surprise." Knowing my father, I thought it could be just about anything. A self-employed jobber, he was always building things out of odds and ends. When we were kids, he once rigged up a jungle gym out of wheels and pulleys. For one of my Halloween parties, he created an electrical pumpkin and mounted it on a broomstick. As guests came to our door, he would light the pumpkin and have it pop out in front of them from a hiding place in the bushes.

Today, however, Dad would say no more, and caught up in the busyness of our new life, I eventually forgot about his surprise.

Until one raw day the following March when I glanced out the window. Dismal. Overcast. Little piles of dirty snow still stubbornly littering the lawn. Would winter ever end?

And yet...was it a mirage? I strained to see what I thought was something pink, miraculously peeking out of a drift. And was that a dot of blue across the yard, a small note of optimism in this gloomy expanse? I grabbed my coat and headed outside for a closer look.

They were crocuses, scattered whimsically throughout the front lawn. Lavender, blue, yellow and my favorite pink—little faces bobbing in the bitter wind.

Dad, I smiled, remembering the bulbs he had secretly planted last fall. He knew how the darkness and dreariness of winter always got me down. What could have been more perfectly timed, more attuned to my needs? How blessed I was, not only for the flowers but for him.

My father's crocuses bloomed each spring for the next four or five seasons, bringing that same assurance every time they arrived: *Hard times almost over. Hold on, keep going, light is coming soon.*

Then a spring came with only half the usual blooms. The next spring there were none. I missed the crocuses, but my life was busier

than ever, and I had never been much of a gardener. I would ask Dad to come over and plant new bulbs. But I never did.

He died suddenly one October day. My family grieved deeply, leaning on our faith. I missed him terribly, though I knew he would always be a part of us.

Four years passed, and on a dismal spring afternoon I was running errands and found myself feeling depressed. You've got the winter blahs again, I told myself. You get them every year; it's chemistry. But it was something else too.

It was Dad's birthday, and I found myself thinking about him. This was not unusual—my family often talked about him, remembering how he lived his faith. Once I saw him take off his coat and give it to a homeless man. Often he'd chat with strangers passing by his storefront, and if he learned they were poor and hungry, he would invite them home for a meal. But now, in the car, I couldn't help wondering, *How* is he now? *Where* is he? Is there really a heaven?

I felt guilty for having doubts, but sometimes, I thought as I turned into our driveway, faith is so hard.

Suddenly I slowed, stopped and stared at the lawn. Muddy grass and small gray mounds of melting snow. And there, bravely waving in the wind, was one pink crocus.

How could a flower bloom from a bulb more than 18 years old, one that had not blossomed in over a decade? But there was the crocus. Tears filled my eyes as I realized its significance.

Hold on, keep going, light is coming soon. The pink crocus bloomed for only a day. But it built my faith for a lifetime.

REPRINTED WITH PERMISSION FROM THE APRIL 1998 *READER'S DIGEST.*

The inner side of every cloud is bright and shining;
I therefore turn my clouds about
And always wear them inside out
To show the lining.
    —Ellen Fowler

SUMMER VACATION
Bruce Larson

FROM *THE ONE AND ONLY YOU*

I have a great friend down in Montgomery, Alabama, and a few years ago he told me an unforgettable story of a summer vacation he had planned for his wife and children. He was unable to go because of business, but he helped them plan every day of a camping trip in the family station wagon from Montgomery all the way to California, up the West Coast, and then back to Montgomery.

He knew their route exactly and the precise time they would be crossing the Great Divide. So, my friend arranged to fly himself out to the nearest airport and hire a car and a driver to take him to a place which every car must pass. He sat by the side of the road several hours waiting for the sight of that familiar station wagon. When it came into view, he stepped out in the road and put his thumb out to hitchhike a ride with the family who assumed that he was 3,000 miles away.

I said to him, "Coleman, I'm surprised they didn't drive off the road in terror or drop dead of a heart attack. What an incredible

story. Why did you go to all that trouble?"

"Well, Bruce," he said, "someday I'm going to be dead, and when that happens, I want my kids and my wife to say, 'You know, Dad was a lot of fun.'"

Wow, I thought. *Here's a man whose whole game plan is to make fun and happiness for other people.* It made me wonder what my own family will remember about me. I'm sure they will say, "Well, Dad was a nice guy but he sure worried a lot about putting out the lights and closing the windows and picking up around the house and cutting the grass." But I'd also like them to be able to say that Dad was the guy who made life a lot of fun.

What sunshine is to flowers, smiles are to humanity.
They are but trifles, to be sure, but scattered along life's pathway,
The good they do is inconceivable.
—Joseph Addison

OUT IN THE FIELDS
WITH GOD

The little cares that fretted me,
I lost them yesterday.
Among the fields above the sea,
Among the winds at play;
Among the lowing of the herds,
The rustling of the trees,
Among the singing of the birds,
The humming of the bees.
The foolish fears of what may happen
I cast them all away
Among the clover-scented grass,
Among the new-mown hay;
Among the husking of the corn
Where drowsy poppies nod,
Where ill thoughts die and good are born,
Out in the fields with God.

Elizabeth Barrett Browning

A MOTHER'S LOVE

David Giannelli

I am a New York City fireman. Being a firefighter has its grim side. When someone's business or home is destroyed, it can break your heart. You see a lot of terror and sometimes even death. But the day I found Scarlett was different. That was a day about life. And love.

It was a Friday. We'd responded to an early morning alarm in Brooklyn at a burning garage. As I was getting my gear on, I heard the sound of cats crying. I couldn't stop—I would have to look for the cats after the fire was put out.

This was a large fire, so there were other hook and ladder companies there as well. We had been told that everyone in the building had made it out safely. I sure hoped so—the entire garage was filled with flames, and it would have been futile for anyone to attempt a rescue anyway. It took a long time and many firefighters to finally bring the enormous blaze under control.

At that point I was free to investigate the cat noises, which I still heard. There continued to be a tremendous amount of smoke and intense heat coming from the building. I couldn't see much, but I

SUNNY MOMENTS

followed the meowing to a spot on the sidewalk about five feet away from the front of the garage. There, crying and huddled together, were three terrified little kittens. Then I found two more, one in the street and one across the street. They must have been in the building, as their fur was badly singed. I yelled for a box and out of the crowd around me, one appeared. Putting the five kittens in the box, I carried them to the porch of a neighboring house. I started looking for a mother cat. It was obvious that the mother had gone into the burning garage and carried each of her babies, one by one, out to the sidewalk. Five separate trips into that raging heat and deadly smoke—it was hard to imagine. Then she had attempted to get them across the street, away from the building. Again, one at a time. But she hadn't been able to finish the job. What had happened to her?

A cop told me he had seen a cat go into a vacant lot near where I'd found the last two kittens. She was there, lying down and crying. She was horribly burnt; her eyes were blistered shut, her paws were blackened, and her fur was singed all over her body. In some places you could see her reddened skin showing through the burnt fur. She was too weak to move anymore. I went over to her slowly, talking gently as I approached. I figured that she was a wild cat and I didn't want to alarm her. When I picked her up, she cried out in pain, but she didn't struggle. The poor animal reeked of burnt fur and flesh.

She gave me a look of utter exhaustion and then relaxed in my arms as much as her pain would allow. Sensing her trust in me, I felt my throat tighten and the tears started in my eyes. I was determined to save this brave little cat and her family. Their lives were, literally, in my hands.

I put the cat in the box with the mewing kittens. Even in her pathetic condition, the blinded mother circled in the box and touched each kitten with her nose, one by one, to make sure they were all there and all safe. She was content, in spite of her pain, now that she was sure the kittens were all accounted for.

These cats obviously needed immediate medical care. I thought of a very special animal shelter out on Long Island, the North Shore Animal League, where I had taken a severely burned dog I had rescued eleven years earlier. If anyone could help them, they could.

I called to alert the Animal League that I was on my way with a badly burned cat and her kittens. Still in my smoke-stained fire gear, I drove my truck there as fast as I could.

When I pulled into the driveway, I saw two teams of vets and technicians standing in the parking lot waiting for me. They whisked the cats into a treatment room—the mother on a table with one vet team and all the kittens on another table with the second team.

Utterly exhausted from fighting the fire, I stood in the treatment room, keeping out of the way. I didn't have much hope that these cats would survive. But somehow, I just couldn't leave them. After a long wait, the vets told me they would observe the kittens and their mother overnight, but they weren't very optimistic about the mother's chances of survival.

I returned the next day and waited and waited. I was about to completely give up hope when the vets finally came over to me. They told me the good news—the kittens would survive.

"And the mother?" I asked. I was afraid to hear the reply. It was still too early to know.

I came back every day, but each day it was the same thing; they just didn't know.

About a week after the fire, I arrived at the shelter in a bleak mood, thinking, *Surely if mother cat was going to make it, she'd have come around by now. How much longer could she hover between life and death?*

But when I walked in the door, the vets greeted me with bright smiles and gave me the thumbs-up sign! Not only was she going to be all right—in time she'd even be able to see again.

Now that she was going to live, she needed a name. One of the technicians came up with the name Scarlett, because of her reddened skin.

Knowing what Scarlett had endured for her kittens, it melted my heart to see her reunited with them. And what did mama cat do first? Another head count! She touched each of her kittens again, nose to nose to be sure they were all still safe and sound. She had risked her life, not once, but five times—and it had paid off. All of her babies had survived.

As a firefighter, I see heroism every day. But what Scarlett showed me that day was the height of heroism—the kind of bravery that comes only from a mother's love.

T H E   D A N C E

Thelda Bevens

F R O M   *A   P A S S A G E   T H R O U G H   G R I E F*

ar and I loved to dance. It was probably the first thing we did together, long before we would share our lives. We grew up in a small Oregon mountain community where dances were held almost every Saturday night, sometimes in the school gym, sometimes at the grange hall, sometimes at the home of Nelson Nye. Nelson and his family loved music and dancing so much that they added a special room to their house large enough to accommodate at least three sets of square dancers. Once a month or more, they invited the entire community to a dance. Nelson played the fiddle and his daughter, Hope, played the piano while the rest of us danced.

In those days, the entire family went together—including the grandparents, the farmers and loggers, the schoolteachers and the store owners. We danced to songs such as "Golden Slippers" and "Red Wing," along with contemporary ones like "Red Sails in the Sunset" and "It's a Sin to Tell a Lie."

Smaller children always had a place to sleep among the coats, close at hand, when they tired. It was a family affair, one of the few entertainments in a small mountain town climbing slowly out of the Great Depression. Dar was seventeen and I was twelve when we first danced. He was one of the best dancers on the floor and so was I. We always jitterbugged. No slow dancing for us, nothing remotely romantic. Our fathers would stand along the wall and watch. They weren't friends. They didn't talk to each other, not even a casual conversation. Both good dancers themselves, they were proud of their kids. Every once in a while, Dar's dad would smile a little, shake his head and say, to no one in particular but so my dad could hear, "Boy, my kid can sure dance."

My dad never blinked an eye; acted like he'd never heard. But a while later he would say, to no one in particular, "That girl of mine can sure dance." And being of the old school, they never told us we were that good or had stirred that tiny bit of boastful rivalry along the wall.

Our dancing together stopped for five years while Dar was in the South Pacific in World War II. During those five years, I grew up. When we met again, Dar was twenty-two and I was almost eighteen. We began to date—and dance again.

This time it was for ourselves—finding our moves, our turns,

our rhythms—adjusting, anticipating, enjoying. We were as good together as we remembered, and this time we added slow dancing to our repertoire.

For us, the metaphor fits. Life is a dance, a movement of rhythms, directions, stumbles, missteps, at times slow and precise, or fast and wild and joyous. We did all the steps.

Two nights before Dar died, the family was with us as they had been for several days—two sons and their wives and four of our eight grandchildren. We all ate dinner together and Dar sat with us. He hadn't been able to eat for several weeks, but he enjoyed it all—told jokes, kidded the boys about their cribbage playing, played with two-year-old Jacob.

Afterward, while the girls were cleaning up the kitchen, I put on a Nat King Cole tape, "Unforgettable." Dar took me in his arms, weak as he was, and we danced.

We held each other and danced and smiled. No tears for us. We were doing what we had loved to do for more than fifty years, and if fate had so ordained, would have gone on doing for fifty more. It was our last dance—forever unforgettable. I wouldn't have missed it for the world.

WHIMSICAL DAYS

LOOKIN' GOOD

Patsy Clairmont

FROM *GOD USES CRACKED POTS*

I remember the day well. It was one of those times when everything goes right. I took a shower and fixed my hair. It went just the way I wanted it to, as it seldom does. I pulled on my new pink sweater, giving me added color, since I need all the help I can get. I pulled on my gray slacks and my taupe heels.

I checked the mirror and thought, *Lookin' good!*

Since it was a cool Michigan day, I slipped on my gray trench coat with pink on the lapels. I was color-coded from head to toe.

When I arrived in downtown Brighton, where I intended to take care of some errands, I was surprised to find heavy traffic. Brighton is a small town, but it has a large health food store. Usually, I can park right in front and run in.

But today business was so brisk I had to park two blocks away. When your attitude is right, and it's a great day, however, inconveniences and interruptions are no big deal.

I thought, *I'll just bounce down the street in time to the sunshine.*

I got out of the car, bounced down the street, crossed the road and entered the store.

As I headed toward the back of the store, I caught my reflection in the glass doors of the refrigeration system. It reaffirmed I was lookin' good. While enjoying my mirrored self, I noticed something was following me. I turned and realized it was my pantyhose!

I remembered the night before when I had done a little Wonder Woman act and taken pantyhose and slacks off in one fell swoop. This morning I put on new pantyhose and must have pushed the old pantyhose through when I pulled on my slacks.

I believe they made their emergence as I bounced down the street in time to the sunshine. I remembered the truck driver who stopped his truck to let me cross. As I looked up, he was laughing, and I thought, *Oh, look! The whole world is happy today!*

So I waved. Little did I realize how much I was waving.

I assumed I had reached some amount of maturity by this time in my life, but I can honestly say that when I looked back and saw that...that...dangling participle, the thought that crossed my mind was, I am going to die!

I knew they were my pantyhose because the right foot was securely wrapped around my ankle. I knew it was secure because I

tried to shake the thing off and pretend I had picked it up in the street.

It's amazing to me that we gals buy these things in flat little packages, we wear them once, and they grow. Now I had a mammoth handful of pantyhose and no place to pitch them. The shelves were crowded with groceries, and my purse was too small and full, so I stuffed them in my coat pocket. They became a protruding hump on my right hip.

I decided to never leave that store. I knew all the store employees in town, and I figured that by now they would have all their employees at the windows waiting for a return parade.

I glanced cautiously around the store and noticed it was Senior Citizens' Day. They were having their blood pressures read, so I got in line to avoid having to leave the store.

The bad news was no one noticed I didn't belong in line. The good news was I had an elevated blood pressure reading. Usually the nurses take mine and say, "I'm sorry but you died two days ago." Today I registered well up the scale.

Finally I realized I'd have to leave. I slipped out the door, down the street, into my car and off for home.

All the way home I said, "I'LL NEVER TELL ANYONE I DID THIS!"

I made it home and got out of the car. My husband was in the yard raking.

I screamed, "Do you know what I did?!"

He was so proud to know his wife had gone through town dragging her underwear. I told him I thought we should move—to another state—in the night. He thought that was extreme and suggested instead that for a while I could walk ten feet behind him. After thinking that through, we decided it should be ten feet in front of him so he could check me out.

If you have ever done anything to embarrass yourself, you know that the more you try not to think about it, the more it comes to you in living color. As I walked through my house, the replay of what I did came to me again and again.

At last I cried out to the Lord, "You take ashes and create beauty, but can You do anything with pantyhose?"

NEW FRIENDS

Teri Leinbaugh

FROM *THE CHRISTIAN READER*

Upon arriving in our new home in Kentucky, my seven-year-old son Jason decided to explore the neighborhood. He was back within the hour proclaiming that he had made some new friends.

"Good. Are they boys or girls?" I asked.

"One is a boy and one is a girl," he replied.

"That's great," I said. "How old are they?"

"Mom," my son replied, almost shocked. "That would be very rude to ask."

I was puzzled at his response. About an hour later, he was back.

"Mom!" my son shouted through the screen door. "I found out how old my new friends are. The girl is 65 and the boy is 70."

GRANDMA'S LAUGHTER

Casandra Lindell

FROM *STORIES FOR THE FAMILY'S HEART*

*V*iolets and roses will always be soft, happy flowers to me because they were my grandmother's favorite—and my grandmother always laughed.

Small pots of violets covered a two-level table in the living room. They must have known she loved them because they were always in bloom. I can see her in my mind's eye, carefully picking off spotted leaves and smiling the flowers from their stems. She did the same thing with people—smiling, encouraging, carefully tending.

Roses bordered the entire yard and Grandma tended them carefully with the same smile. Throughout the spring and summer Grandpa regularly cut armfuls of roses for the house. He kept the tables full of bouquets in cut glass vases. Any visitor could count on taking home a handful of roses from the yard.

But visitors took home more than roses—they took home Grandma's laughter. She "got tickled" when she was lost and drove in circles looking for an address. She smiled with warmth to match the main course as she put the last of the evening meal on the table.

She laughed in delight as she cuddled me while I told her a story. She giggled when hummingbirds fluttered outside the dining room window.

When Grandma dropped a glass bottle of maple syrup in the grocery store, she smiled and said she felt clumsy. She turned to call someone to clean it up and stepped in the syrup. She slipped and fell and broke her wrist. As she lay there on her back, propped on her unbroken arm to keep from lying on a shard of glass, Grandma started laughing. She laughed while the employees helped her up. She laughed as she waited for the ambulance, and she laughed when she told the story even years later.

When she died, my five-year-old nephew wanted to say good-bye, and he didn't quite understand what that meant. My sister told him, the best she could, that he wouldn't be able to sit in Grandma's lap and she wouldn't tell him stories anymore. Tommy drew a picture and his dad helped him write "I'll miss you, Grandma. It's okay to cry" across the top.

"Mommy?" His big eyes were questioning, his brow puzzled. "I won't hear her laughing, will I?"

Like Tommy, I thought I would miss Grandma's laughter most of all.

Until four months later. I sat at Grandma's dining room table, painting a vase as I waited for Grandpa to come home. As I reached to pick up the phone, my sleeve caught the container of black paint and swept it off the table—to land upside down on the carpet.

"That's okay," I heard myself say out loud in a sweet and gentle tone not quite my own. "Clean it up as best you can. It's an old carpet." And then I started laughing. I laughed at my clumsiness and at the black smear that just seemed to spread despite my best efforts. I giggled at the mass of paper towels piling up in the garbage bag. And then I sat back and laughed in delight at a full grown little girl who had learned to *find* delight in even the messiest situations.

I almost looked up to see if Grandma was standing there—and then I realized that Grandma's laughter was still with me.

Wrinkles should merely indicate where smiles have been.
— Mark Twain

HAPPY TIMES

Be glad of life,

because it gives you the chance

to love and to work and to play

and to look up at the stars.

Henry Van Dyke

ICE CREAM

Joe LoMusio

FROM *IF I SHOULD DIE BEFORE I LIVE*

tourist was standing in line to buy an ice cream cone at a Thrifty Drug store in Beverly Hills. To her utter shock and amazement, who should walk in and stand right behind her but Paul Newman! Well the lady, even though she was rattled, determined to maintain her composure. She purchased her ice cream cone and turned confidently and exited the store.

However, to her horror, she realized that she had left the counter without her ice cream cone! She waited a few minutes till she felt all was clear, and then went back into the store to claim her cone. As she approached the counter, the cone was not in the little circular receptacle, and for a moment she stood there pondering what might have happened to it. Then she felt a polite tap on her shoulder, and turning was confronted by—you guessed it—Paul Newman. The famous actor then told the lady that if she was looking for her ice cream cone, she had put it into her purse!

JUST ONE KISS!

Susan Wales

FROM *A MATCH MADE IN HEAVEN*

Mr. Baumann's doctors had warned him and his wife that he was at high risk for a heart attack. But when the attack actually came, Mrs. Baumann still wasn't prepared. Gripped with shock, fear, and panic, she rode by her husband's side in the ambulance, repeatedly crying out to God to save him.

At the hospital, the nurses had to pull Mrs. Baumann away from her husband so the doctors could examine him. After they had successfully stabilized his heart, Mrs. Baumann rushed down the hall to the telephones to call each of their seven children. With tears of exhaustion and relief, she told them of their father's heart attack, assuring them that his condition was now stable.

But when Mrs. Baumann returned to her husband's room, she gasped at the sight before her. Two nurses stood over her husband. Tubes ran in and out of his trembling body, and machines and monitors were humming and beeping. His face was bright red, and he was gasping for breath.

"What have you done to my husband?" she cried.

One of the nurses explained, as sympathetically as possible, that he had suffered a massive stroke.

A stroke! On top of the heart attack! Mrs. Baumann couldn't control her emotions. Overcome with grief and blinded by tears, she grabbed her husband's head off the pillow. She held him tightly in her arms, calling out his name and kissing his lips.

At that very moment, the doctor walked in and demanded, "Mrs. Baumann, what do you think you're doing?"

She turned to the doctor and hotly declared, "The question is, Doctor, what have you done to my husband?"

The doctor shook his head and chuckled, "Mrs. Baumann, that is not your husband!"

For a moment, Mrs. Baumann was so stunned she couldn't speak. Then she looked more carefully at the man on the bed.

"He's...he's...not!" she cried, turning a dark shade of crimson. "Oh no! Oh dear! Oh no!"

Gently a nurse escorted the mortified Mrs. Baumann out into the hall.

"Why didn't that man try to stop me?" asked Mrs. Baumann.

"Because of his stroke, he's unable to move or to speak," the nurse answered.

Mrs. Baumann gasped. "And now he must be wondering

why that strange lady kissed him!"

As soon as they entered her husband's room, Mrs. Baumann rushed to her husband's side and kissed him. Then, still very shaken, she related her mistake. "He had so many tubes and...and...I hope I didn't hurt him, Bernie!"

Mr. Baumann smiled and assured his wife that the man was probably feeling better than ever. But Mrs. Baumann decided she better go down to the chapel to pray for both Bernie and the man she'd kissed—and perhaps made worse!

A few days later the doctor dropped by Mr. Baumann's room for his final checkup. "Mrs. Baumann," he said, "you'll be glad to know that your husband and my patient across the hall have both made miraculous recoveries. Do you suppose it was my good doctoring, your prayers, or your passionate kisses?"

"Why, why..." she fumbled.

"Maybe it was all three!" the doctor added with a wink.

LEGEND OF THE
FORGET-ME-NOTS

When to the flowers so beautiful

the Father gave a name,

there came a little blue-eyed one—

all timidly it came.

And standing at the Father's feet,

and gazing in His face,

it said with low and timid voice,

and yet with gentle grace,

"Dear Lord, the name Thou gavest me,

alas, I have forgot."

The Father kindly looked on him

and said, "Forget-me-not."

Author unknown

THE RING BEARER

Dennis Kizziar

RETOLD BY MATTHEW L. JACOBSON

FROM *STORIES FOR THE FAMILY'S HEART*

*J*ohnny was very excited. It was the first time he had ever been asked to do something this important. As the wedding music began to play he imagined just how he should carry the pillow with two shiny rings tied on top. Just before touching him on the shoulder to give him the cue to walk down the aisle, his mother looked down and smiled into the upturned face of her four-year-old son. "Don't worry, Mommy." Johnny implored, "I'll do a good job."

Then Johnny took a deep breath, furrowed his brow, bared his teeth and said "Grrrrrrr!" Everyone turned to face the back of the church. Where was that strange noise coming from?

Johnny growled all the louder and much to Mrs. Smith's surprise, who was sitting on the third pew from the back, he ran up to her and struck her feathered hat with the pillow. His mother looked on in horror. Johnny was fast. He ran back and forth from pew to pew growling and making menacing faces.

Upon reaching the front of the church, Johnny composed himself and gently held up the pillow so the pastor, nonplussed at the performance, could remove the rings. The rest of the ceremony went off without a hitch.

During the reception, the pastor walked up to Johnny who was getting his second piece of wedding cake. "Say, Johnny, what were you doing while bringing the rings to me?"

"My job," declared Johnny proudly. "They asked me to be the Ring Bear!"

Take time to laugh—it is the music of the soul.

— Anonymous

THE JEWELRY BOX
Faith Andrews Bedford

FROM *MARY ENGELBREIT'S HOME COMPANION*

*T*onight is our anniversary and my husband is taking me out. I look through my closet and pick out a deep green velvet dress with long sleeves and a high neck. It looks wonderful with my mother's seed pearl necklace and my grandmother's tiny pearl earrings.

As I sit at my dressing table, my daughter, Eleanor, perches beside. She loves to watch me get dressed for special occasions. "Mama," she addresses my reflection in the mirror, "may I pick out your jewelry?"

"Of course," I reply.

She opens the drawer where I keep my jewelry box and begins to sift through the contents. There are the macaroni necklaces she made me in kindergarten and the locket my husband gave me when we were engaged. In a little box Eleanor finds my old Girl Scout pin and some badges.

She holds several pairs of earrings up to her small ears, then discards them. She tries on several necklaces, and shakes her head. At last, with a little cry of delight, she pounces on a pair of long,

dangly earrings from Ceylon. They are set with flashing mirrors, obviously left over from the seventies. I wore them with bell-bottoms and tunics. In another box she finds two long ropes of beads from the same era.

She drapes the beads around my neck and hands me the earrings. I put them on and give my head a little shake. The earrings glitter brightly.

"Perfect!" She sighs with pleasure. We grin at each other in the mirror.

As Eleanor twirls out of the room to tell her father that I am almost ready, I remember how, when I was Eleanor's age, I used to watch, entranced, as my own mother prepared for an evening out.

While she pinned up her French twist, I would ask her to tell me where each piece had come from.

In a velvet case lay a beautiful garnet necklace and matching earrings. Mother told me that they belonged to her grandmother who wore them to Boston, where she had seen the famous Sarah Bernhardt perform.

The seed pearl necklace had been given to Mother by her godmother as a wedding present. Like me, she always wore it with the tiny pearl earrings her grandmother left her. Now I have inherited both.

My favorite things in the drawer were the gifts my father had

given her. In a velvet box was a necklace of rhinestones that glittered with the brilliance of real diamonds. Mother told me they were not diamonds at all, but I thought she still looked like a princess.

When Father went on a business trip to Arizona, he brought Mother back a ring with a big square piece of turquoise. It just fit her ring finger; it was too big for my thumb.

For her fortieth birthday, he presented her with some earrings from India. The black enamel had been cut away to reveal silver figures of dancing women bent into impossible positions. My sisters and I tried to imitate them. We couldn't.

The Christmas I was ten I had saved up enough money to buy Mother some earrings at the five and dime: two red plastic bells hung from tiny bows. The edges had been sprinkled with silver glitter. Mother wore them all Christmas day. She shook her head frequently to show us how they actually made a tinkling sound.

A few days later, I came into her room just in time to help zip up her black and white taffeta evening dress.

"Will you pick out some earrings for me, dear?" she asked.

Opening her drawer I sorted through the options. Her dress was pretty, I thought, but it needed a bit of color. I proudly pulled out the little red plastic bells.

"Just the thing," she said, putting them on. I looked at her and thought no one ever was more beautiful.

My husband's voice pulls me back to the present. "Ready?" he asks.

"Almost," I reply, putting Mother's pearls and Grandmother's earrings back into my jewelry box.

As I come down the stairs, my beads swinging and the brass earrings flashing in the light, I look down and see Eleanor's proud face. "You look beautiful," she sighs.

"Only with your help," I reply as I kiss her good night. She will be asleep by the time I return.

❧

I will go pick daisies and have a happy heart.
—*Kimber Annie Engstrom*

SPLASHES OF ENCOURAGEMENT

By the Way, My Name Is Joe

Author unknown

*H*e was driving home one evening on a two-lane country road. Ever since the Levi's factory closed, he'd been unemployed, but he'd never quit looking. Now with winter raging, the chill had finally hit home.

It was a lonely road. He could go down this road blind and tell you what was on either side, and with his headlights not working, that came in handy. It was getting dark and the snow flurries had started.

He almost didn't see the old lady stranded on the side of the road. He could see she needed help. So he pulled his sputtering old car up in front of her Mercedes and got out. Even with the smile on his face, she was worried. No one had stopped to help for the last hour. Was he going to hurt her? He didn't look safe—he looked poor and hungry. He could see that she was frightened and cold. He knew how she felt. He said, "I'm here to help you, ma'am. Why don't you wait in my car where it's warm. By the way, my name is Joe."

Well, all she had was a flat tire, but for an older lady, that was bad enough. Joe skinned his knuckles a time or two setting up the

jack. His bare hands were so cold he didn't feel it. Soon the tire was changed. As he put the jack away in the trunk, she came back to her car, warmed and calmed. She told Joe that she was from St. Louis and was on her way home. She thanked him and asked how much she owed him. Joe just smiled as he closed the trunk.

Any amount would have been all right with her. She had already imagined all the awful things that could have happened had he not stopped. Joe never thought twice about the money. This was not a job to him. This was helping someone in need and God knows there were plenty who had given him a hand in the past. He had lived his whole life that way and it never occurred to him to act any other way. He told her that if she really wanted to pay him back, the next time she saw someone who needed help, she could give that person the assistance that they needed, and Joe added, "and think of me."

A few miles down the road the lady saw a small café. She went in to grab a bite to eat and take the chill off before making the last part of her trip. It was a dingy looking place. Outside were two old gas pumps. Neither the cash register or the telephone rang very often.

The waitress brought her a clean towel to wipe the snow from

her head and face. She had a sweet smile even after being on her feet all day. And she was eight months pregnant, but she never let the strain change her attitude. The old lady wondered how someone who had so little could be so giving to a stranger. Then she remembered Joe.

After the lady finished her meal, and the waitress went to get her change from the hundred dollar bill, she slipped right out the door. When the waitress returned to the table she noticed something written on the napkin. It said, "You don't owe me a thing. I've been there too. Someone once helped me out the way I'm helping you. If you want to pay me back, here's what you do. Don't let the chain of love end with you."

Well, that night when the waitress got home from work and climbed into bed, she thought about the money and what the lady had written. How could she have known how much she and her husband needed it? With the baby due next month, it was going to be hard. She knew how worried her husband was, and as he lay sleeping next to her, she gave him a soft kiss and whispered soft and low, "Everything's gonna be all right. I love you, Joe."

LOVE NOTES
Dale Hanson Bourke
FROM *EVERYDAY MIRACLES*

*S*o *you're* the one who started all the trouble!" the well-dressed woman said to me as I introduced myself. I looked at her blankly. Standing in the middle of our children's classroom, I couldn't imagine what she was talking about.

"The notes," she declared. "I mean the notes in the children's lunchboxes. Because of your son, all the children have to have them now."

My mouth dropped open as I listened to her. I had no idea anyone even knew about the notes I tucked into Chase's lunchbox each day. But apparently he had shown them to his friends, who asked their mothers for notes, too.

I usually did my son's notes late at night before I fell into bed, or early in the morning before anyone else was awake. Blurry-eyed, I drew pictures or wrote simple words that Chase would recognize. These communiqués were my way of helping him make it through his long school day. So at lunchtime I tried to give him a little extra boost to remind him that he was special.

Now I realized the notes *had* made a difference for Chase. He felt so good about them that he had shown them to his friends. And they all wanted to feel special as well.

Each night when I cleaned out Chase's lunchbox, I would find the day's note, with greasy little fingerprints on it. It made me smile to think of him reading his note each day as he ate his lunch.

One day I opened his lunchbox to find only crumbs and a half-eaten carrot. "Where's your note, Chase?" I asked.

He looked sheepish. "Sorry, Mom," he said. "I gave it to Jimmy."

"Why?"

"Well, he never gets a note. So I thought I could share mine with him." Chase looked at me sideways, waiting for my reaction.

He was relieved when I bent down and hugged him. Jimmy's mom was single and worked long hours to support her family. I was proud my son passed his precious note on to Jimmy.

"You're a very special boy," I told him.

"I know," he responded.

All I could do was laugh. I had thought that Chase needed a note each day to remind him of that fact. Instead, he was reminding his classmates through his kindness. More importantly, he was reminding me.

LUTHER'S LUMBER
Joe Edwards

*L*uther had been home from the war nearly four months, now, and worked at the Carnation Milk plant in Mount Vernon where his wife, Jenny, worked.

This morning he was in the little Miller café next door to the post office waiting for the mail to be "put up." Sitting across from him in the booth was his old friend, Fred Hill. They were discussing the war which was still going on in the Pacific theater. Recruitment posters still lined the walls of the little café.

Fred had not been in the service, because when the war started in 1941, his parents had been in very poor health; his father with a bad heart, and his mother with cancer. He was needed at home to care for them and operate the farm. His parents had since died, and the farm was now his—his and Maggie's.

When Luther, Fred's best friend since childhood, had flown over Miller in the B-17, and when the bodies of the Hobbs boys and Billie Martin had been shipped home, and when Perry came home with hooks where his hands should have been, Fred felt guilty. He felt he had not done his part for the war effort, and in

his own eyes, he was diminished.

But today, it was Luther who seemed depressed. Fred asked him what was bothering him. "You seem down in the dumps today, Luther," he said. "I can't see what could be botherin' you. You came through the war without a scratch; you got a beautiful wife and a baby on the way; you got a good job. What's the problem?"

"Jenny's mother is in bad shape," said Luther, "We're going to have to take her in, and with the baby coming we don't have the room."

"Can't build a room on?" asked Fred.

"No lumber available," said Luther. "I've tried here, and Mount Vernon, Springfield, Joplin, and there won't be any more shipments for the duration. Who knows how long that will be?"

"Tried Will's sawmill?"

"Yeah, but he just saws oak, and it's green. The baby'll be here in August, and we can't wait for the lumber to dry. Besides, you can't build a whole room out of oak, anyway."

"Wouldn't want to," said Fred, "Reckon the mail's up?"

"Probably."

The two young men left the café and went into the post office next door. Buford Patten, the postmaster, had raised the door to the service window, signaling that the mail was in the boxes. Luther and

Fred retrieved their mail and left—Luther to work at Mount Vernon, and Fred back to the farm.

That evening, Fred finished the milking and sat on the front porch with Maggie. "Days are getting longer," he said, "Man could get half a day's work done after five o'clock."

"Better put your pa's car up," said Maggie. "Radio says rain tonight."

Fred's father had bought a new 1941 Ford just before his first heart attack, and the car was now Fred's. He had built a new garage for it just before Christmas, and tonight he congratulated himself on getting it built before the lumber ran out. He didn't even know it had until Luther told him this morning.

Fred drove the car into the new garage and latched the door. He walked back around the house to the front porch. Something was nagging at his mind, but he couldn't define it. He shook it off and sat on the porch with Maggie until darkness fell. They could see heat lightning in the west, and the wind started to rise. They went in the house to listen to the news of the war on the radio, and shortly went to bed.

The next morning, Fred again drove his pickup into Miller for the mail. The air was fresh and clear now, the rain having washed it clean. The sun was shining, and he felt good. When he reached the

café, Luther was there ahead of him.

"Still haven't found any lumber, I guess?"

"No, I asked everybody at work, and nobody knows of any. I don't know what we'll do."

Now the nagging in Fred's mind defined itself. "I found the lumber for you," he said.

"You did? Where?" Luther was delighted.

"Fella I know. He'll let you have it free, you bein' a veteran and all. He doesn't seem to want you to know who he is, so I'll have to haul it in for you. It's good lumber, fir and pine, cut different lengths and got nails in it, but that's no problem. Tell you what, you get your foundation poured, and I'll bring you a pickup load every day and help you build it. We'll have it done before the baby gets here."

"That's a friend for you," Luther said to himself, as he drove to Mount Vernon. That evening he came home with sacks of cement in his pickup.

Luther dug and poured the foundation, and when it was ready for the footings, he told Fred.

"Fine," said Fred. "I'll bring the first load over and be there when you get home from work."

Fred appeared every evening with a load of lumber, and the two

men worked until it was too dark to see. Sometimes Maggie came too, and the women sat in the house listening to the radio or talking about babies or Jenny's ailing mother, their sentences punctuated by the sound of the hammers outside.

Over the next few weeks the new room took shape and was finished and roofed. "Where did you get the shingles?" asked Luther.

"Same fella," answered Fred. "He's got all kinds of stuff."

Luther didn't push. Lots of older folks liked to help out the young veterans anonymously. It was common.

It was done! The women fixed the room up inside, and moved Jenny's mother in. The men went back about their business.

At supper one evening, Luther told Jenny he would like to do something nice for Fred and Maggie, since they had been so helpful with the new room.

"I know," said Jenny brightly. "Maggie likes those big wooden lawn chairs like Aunt Birdie has in her lawn. Why not get them a couple of those?"

"Good idea," agreed Luther, and the next Saturday he bought a couple at Callison's hardware and loaded them into his pickup.

When he got out to Fred's farm, there was no one home, Fred and Maggie having gone into Springfield, shopping. *That's okay,* Luther thought, *I'll just put them in the garage in case it rains.*

He drove around the house and into the driveway that led to Fred's new garage.

The garage was gone. Only the foundation remained to show where it had been.

Luther put the chairs on the front porch and drove home, tears in his eyes.

The two men are now in their midseventies and are still the best of friends. They never spoke of the incident.

How could they? There was nothing to say.

Keep your face to the sunshine and you cannot see the shadow.
—*Helen Keller*

GARDENERS OF THE SOUL

Let us be grateful to people

who make us happy;

they are the charming gardeners

who make our souls blossom.

Marcel Proust

M O L L Y

Barbara Baumgardner

FROM *HUMANE SOCIETY OF CENTRAL OREGON* NEWSLETTER

When I take Molly for a walk, I frequently get waylaid by people who "once had a golden retriever." I call them *kindred hearts* because they don't seem to object as Molly leaves hair and drool all over their pant legs whenever I stop to chat. *Kindred hearts* are a lot more tolerant of things like shaggy, shedding, slobbering dogs—and of people, too, in general. Molly is learning to pick out those kindred hearts when we go visiting the nursing homes, assisted living centers, and hospitals.

At 18 months old, I wasn't sure she would be able to calm down enough to be a "visiting dog" under the Humane Society program. She is a typical golden: affectionate but active, tail-wagging, always ready to play. Tom Davis described her well in his book, *Just Goldens,* when he said, "Goldens are imaginative, mellow, enemies of rout…quirky, fun-loving and full of surprises…you'd want a Golden to throw a party. A couple of hours into the festivities, it's the one wearing the lampshade."

That's Molly: the one wearing the lampshade.

She wasn't sure what her role was when we began to make our scheduled visits. She'd wiggle and whop everyone around her with her tail; the tail that wags with such force it can hurt or it can clear the coffee table. She thinks she is still a lap dog but we weren't visiting anyone healthy and big enough to hold her. However, like all goldens, she has that innate desire to please me. As I coached, she finally figured out that if she would sit, someone would pet her or better yet, hug her. And sometimes she would lay her head in a willing lap.

Recently on one of our visits, she performed like a pro. We were at a health care center, in the section where people need a lot of care. A woman, secured to a wheelchair, seemed so unaware that we nearly passed her by. Her hands were crippled and bent under; her head had fallen to one side, eyes closed. Molly paused and so did I.

The woman responded to my touch when I put my hand on her arm so I grasped a gnarled hand and touched it to Molly's soft fur. As her hand in mine stroked Molly's head, the woman opened her eyes and began to laugh. Soon she was alert, but giggling like a child as I continued to move her hand around the golden's body. Molly sat close, and soon put her head on the lap in the wheelchair.

Then with her own strength, the woman managed to bend forward enough to push her arms around Molly's neck, her excited giggles catching the attention of the nurses close by. The woman couldn't speak, but she communicated her kindred heart: giving love through touch, in the same way Molly does.

My dog and I will return to visit the woman again. I think Molly finally understands that when she's on assignment, she must give up the lampshade and just be the light.

*The best way to cheer yourself up is
to try to cheer somebody else up.*
—Mark Twain

LONGER, DADDY...LONGER!
Gary Smalley and John Trent
FROM *LEAVING THE LIGHT ON*

*R*ecently, a woman grabbed my arm at a conference after I had finished speaking on the enormous need we all have for affirmation.

"Dr. Trent, may I tell you my story?" she asked. "Actually, it's a story of something my son did with my granddaughter that illustrates what you've been talking about—the importance of affirmation.

"My son has two daughters, one who's five and one who is in the 'terrible twos.'" When a grandmother says this child is in the "terrible twos," believe me, she is!

"For several years, my son has taken the oldest girl out for a 'date' time, but he had never taken the two-year-old until recently. On his first 'date' with the younger one, he took her out to breakfast at a local fast-food restaurant.

"They had just gotten their pancakes and my son decided it would be a good time to tell this child how much he loved and appreciated her."

"Jenny," her son had said, "I want you to know how much I love you, and how special you are to Mom and me. We prayed for you for years, and now that you're here and growing up to be such a wonderful girl, we couldn't be more proud of you."

Once he had said all this, he stopped talking and reached over for his fork to begin eating...but he never got the fork to his mouth.

His daughter reached out her little hand and laid it on her father's hand. His eyes went to hers, and in a soft, pleading voice she said, "Longer, Daddy...longer."

He put down his fork and proceeded to tell her some more reasons and ways they loved and appreciated her, and then he again reached for his fork. A second time...and a third...and a fourth time he heard the words, "Longer, Daddy...longer."

This father never did get much to eat that morning, but his daughter got the emotional nourishment she needed so much. In fact, a few days later, she spontaneously ran up to her mother and said, "I'm a really special daughter, Mommy. Daddy told me so."

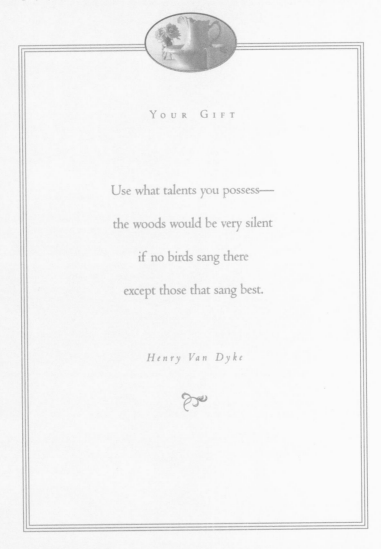

YOUR GIFT

Use what talents you possess—

the woods would be very silent

if no birds sang there

except those that sang best.

Henry Van Dyke

THE GIFT OF GAB

Lynn Rogers Petrak

Although she told me not to talk to strangers, my mother always did. At the checkout line. Browsing through handbags at Marshall Field. During a slow elevator ride, when everyone else was seriously squinting at the buttons. At airports, football games, and the beach.

Thankfully, I only took her advice when it came to menacing strangers. I believe I'm better for it.

My mother's habit of striking up conversations with people next to her may bring a smile to my eyes now, but it proved rather embarrassing during my tender teenage years. "Lynn's getting her first one, too," she confided to a woman also shopping with her adolescent daughter in the bra section of our hometown department store. I contemplated running and hiding under a nearby terry cloth bathrobe, but instead I turned crimson and hissed "Mothhhhherrrrr" between gritted teeth. I felt only slightly better when the girl's mother said, "We're trying to find one for Sarah, but they're all too big."

Not everyone responded when Mom made an observation and tried to spark a brief discussion. Some people gave her a tight-lipped half-grin, then turned away. A few completely ignored her. Whenever I was with her during those times, I could see that she was a little hurt, but she'd shrug it off and we'd continue on our way.

More often than not, however, I would wander off somewhere and come back to find her gabbing away. There were occasions when I was concerned that I'd lost her in the crowd, but then I'd hear her singsong laugh and a comment like, "Yes, yes, me too."

Through these spontaneous chats, my mother taught me that our world is much too large—or too small, take your pick—not to have time to reach out to one another. She reminded me that as women, we enjoy a special kind of kinship, even if we're really not all that alike. In the most mundane things, there are common threads that bind us. It may be the reason we like paper versus plastic, or why a navy sweater is never a bad buy, or why the national anthem still gives us goose bumps.

One of the last memories of my mother, when she was in the hospital and a few hours from dying from the breast cancer that had ravaged her down to 85 pounds, is of her smiling weakly and talking to her nurse about how to best plant tulip bulbs. I stood silently

in the doorway, wanting to cry but feeling such a surge of love and warmth. She taught me to see spring in others. I'll never forget it, especially now when I turn to someone and say, "Don't you just love it when…"

Plant a word of love heart-deep in a person's life.
Nurture it with a smile and a
prayer and watch what happens.
— M a x   L u c a d o

LIFTED

Rochelle M. Pennington

*G*ramps was a talker since the day he was born, and at the ripe old age of eightyish, practice had certainly made perfect. Easy-flowing conversations had always kept him in the thick of things; exactly where he liked to be.

His daily rounds led him through town in a predictable manner: post office, café, hardware store, grocery mart—and pretty much in that order. Since he preferred getting his news from people rather than from the papers, this could be accomplished easily enough while "out and about" among the locals. He'd return home midafternoon quite satisfied that he had a handle on the world: what was new, what was old, and what was in between.

Today was not unlike any other day, with Gramps making his final stop at the grocery store to pick up a loaf of bread before heading home. That's when he spotted them: the nonlocals. A mother with two small children had just rounded the corner of the aisle. There wasn't anything Gramps enjoyed quite so much as striking up small talk with someone he had never met before. Forgetting that he had been reaching for a loaf of bread, Gramps shifted gears

from Grocery Shopper into Public Relations Specialist. The process of de-strangerization took less than eight minutes after which Gramps knew that they had just moved to town, were living on Elm Street in the blue Cape Cod on the corner, were celebrating the father's birthday this afternoon, and had come to purchase a bouquet of balloons for the party. "A birthday party, you say!" Gramps cheerfully exclaimed as he quickly joined into their circle of anticipated excitement. It was a nice place to be.

Always helpful, Gramps walked along with them to the back corner of the store where the helium tank and balloon display were located. A rainbow of colored balloons were chosen, inflated, and tied together with curled ribbons. "Wait till Daddy sees this!" chirped the children's soprano voices.

Both Gramps and the little family were soon ready to check out. Since Mabel's line was open, they filed in: skipping girls in pink dresses first, mother carrying white purse next, Gramps and his bread last of all. Being a mother of seven and the purchaser of many dozen balloon bouquets over the years herself—some of which made it to their intended recipient and most of which simply floated away instead—Mabel felt it her maternal duty to gently share some reminders. "Such wonderful balloons you have! Why, there's so many of them I should think they would just lift the both

of you up together like Mary Poppins!" Giggles. "Now you better hang on tight. Real tight. Gramps told me you're on your way to a birthday party. We want those balloons to get there, right?" In response, four chubby little hands clenched the strings even tighter.

Gramps and Mabel shouted departing greetings to the family as they left. "Have fun! Remember to hang on tight! We'll be seeing you soon!" Placing his bread upon the conveyor belt, Gramps continued to watch them through the large wall of windows as they walked outside. No sooner had they gotten beyond the expansive overhang of the building than the clenched hands were opened and the balloons lifted. Gramps wailed, "Oh, no!" as he went darting out the door with the agility of a track star. Upon reaching them he continued to lament, but no one seemed to hear. His words were drowned out by the usual reaction of children in the presence of helium balloons set free: little voices squealing, little hearts laughing, little hands clapping, and little feet jumping for joy as they watched the bouquet dance across the endless sky in freedom. Although a natural reaction—a predictable reaction—these little ones seemed to have an added exuberance. *Ah, youth*, thought Gramps.

Touching their mother's shoulder gently, Gramps was going to offer to spring for the next bouquet. "Too bad about the balloons.

They're supposed to be for their father."

Touching Gramps's shoulder gently in return, the young woman responded, "And he'll be receiving them anytime soon now...in heaven."

Never before—or since—has Gramps attended a birthday party quite so splendid.

VALENTINES
Dale Galloway
FROM *DREAM A NEW DREAM*

Little Chad was a shy, quiet young fella. One day he came home and told his mother he'd like to make a valentine for everyone in his class. Her heart sank. She thought, *I wish he wouldn't do that!* because she had watched the children when they walked home from school. Her Chad was always behind them. They laughed and hung on to each other and talked to each other. But Chad was never included. Nevertheless, she decided she would go along with her son. So she purchased the paper and glue and crayons. For three whole weeks, night after night, Chad painstakingly made thirty-five valentines.

Valentine's Day dawned, and Chad was beside himself with excitement! He carefully stacked them up, put them in a bag, and bolted out the door. His mom decided to bake him his favorite cookies and serve them up warm and nice with a cool glass of milk when he came home from school. She just knew he would be disappointed...maybe that would ease the pain a little. It hurt her to think that he wouldn't get many valentines—maybe none at all.

That afternoon she had the cookies and milk on the table. When she heard the children outside she looked out the window. Sure enough here they came, laughing and having the best time. And, as always, there was Chad in the rear. He walked a little faster than usual. She fully expected him to burst into tears as soon as he got inside. His arms were empty, she noticed, and when the door opened she choked back the tears.

"Mommy has some warm cookies and milk for you."

But he hardly heard her words. He just marched right on by, his face aglow, and all he could say was:

"Not a one...not a one."

Her heart sank.

And then he added, "I didn't forget a one, not a single one!"

THE STUDENT'S MITE
David R. Collins

FROM *TEACHERS IN FOCUS* MAGAZINE

*T*he situation seemed hopeless. From the first day he entered my seventh-grade classroom, Willard P. Franklin had existed in his own world, shutting out his classmates and me, his teacher. My attempts at establishing a friendly relationship were met with complete indifference. Even a "Good morning, Willard" received only an inaudible grunt. His classmates fared no better. Willard was strictly a loner, finding no desire or need to lower the barrier of silence he had erected. His clothes were clean—but definitely not on the cutting edge of style. He could have been a trendsetter because his outfits possessed a "hand-me-down" look before such a look was in.

Shortly after the Thanksgiving holidays, we received an announcement regarding the annual Christmas collection.

"Christmas is a season of giving," I told my students. "There are a few students in the school who might not have a happy holiday season. By contributing to our Christmas collection, you will

help to buy food, clothing and toys for these needy people. You may bring your money tomorrow."

When I called for the contributions the next day, I discovered everyone had forgotten—everyone except Willard P. Franklin. The boy dug deep into his pants pockets as he strolled up to my desk. Carefully he dropped a nickel into the small container.

"I don't need no milk for lunch," he mumbled. For a moment, just a moment, he smiled. I watched him turn and walk back to his desk.

That night, after school, I took our meager contribution—one lone nickel—to the school principal. I couldn't help telling him the giver's identity and sharing with him the incident.

"I may be wrong, but I believe Willard may be ready to become a part of the world around him," I told the principal.

"Yes, I believe it sounds hopeful," he nodded. "And I have a hunch we might profit from him letting us share a bit of his world. I just received a list of the poor families of our school who most need help through the Christmas collection. Here, look at it."

And as I gazed down to read, I discovered Willard P. Franklin and his family were the top names on the list.

I LOVE YOU ANYWAY

Dr. Joe Harding

It was Friday morning and a young businessman finally decided to ask his boss for a raise. Before leaving for work, he told his wife what he was about to do. All day long he felt nervous and apprehensive. Finally in the late afternoon he summoned the courage to approach his employer, and to his delight, the boss agreed to the raise.

The elated husband arrived home to a beautiful table set with their best china and lighted candles. Smelling the aroma of a festive meal, he figured that someone from the office had called his wife and tipped her off! Finding her in the kitchen, he eagerly shared the details of his good news. They embraced and danced around the room before sitting down to the wonderful meal his wife had prepared. Next to his plate he found an artistically lettered note that read, "Congratulations, darling! I knew you'd get the raise! This dinner is to show you how much I love you."

Later on his way to the kitchen to help his wife serve dessert, he noticed that a second card had fallen from her pocket. Picking it

up off the floor, he read, "Don't worry about not getting the raise! You deserve it anyway! This dinner is to show how much I love you."

Total acceptance! Total love. She stood behind him no matter what—softening the blows, healing the wounds, and believing in him. We can be rejected by many if we're loved by one.

TREASURES OF INSPIRATION

COMING HOME
David Redding

FROM *JESUS MAKES ME LAUGH*

I remember going home from the Navy for the first time during World War II. Home was so far out in the country that when we went hunting we had to go toward town. We had moved there for my father's health when I was just 13. We raised cattle and sheep.

I started a little flock of Shropshire sheep, the kind that are completely covered by wool except for a black nose and the tips of black legs. My father helped them have their twins at lambing time, and I could tell each one of the flock apart at a distance with no trouble. I had a beautiful ram. Next door was a poor man who had a beautiful dog and a small flock of sheep he wanted to improve with my ram. He asked me if he could borrow the ram; in return he would let me have the choice of the litter from his prize dog.

That is how I got Teddy, a big, black Scottish shepherd. Teddy was my dog, and he would do anything for me. He waited for me to come home from school. He slept beside me, and when I whistled he ran to me even if he were eating. At night no one could

get within a half mile without Teddy's permission. During those long summers in the fields I would only see the family at night, but Teddy was with me all the time. And so when I went away to war, I didn't know how to leave him. How do you explain to someone who loves you that you are leaving him and will not be chasing woodchucks with him tomorrow like always?

So, coming home that first time from the Navy was something I can scarcely describe. The last bus stop was fourteen miles from the farm. I got off there that night at about eleven o'clock and walked the rest of the way home. It was two or three in the morning before I was within a half mile of the house. It was pitch dark, but I knew every step of the way. Suddenly Teddy heard me and began his warning bark. Then I whistled only once. The barking stopped. There was a yelp of recognition, and I knew that a big black form was hurtling toward me in the darkness. Almost immediately he was there in my arms. To this day that is the best way I can explain what I mean by coming home.

What comes home to me now is the eloquence with which that unforgettable memory speaks to me of my God. If my dog, without any explanation, would love me and take me back after all that time, wouldn't my God?

S O W I N G   L O V E

Gladys Hunt

F R O M   *D O E S   A N Y O N E   H E R E   K N O W   G O D ?*

The neighbors in the little house next door were a sorry lot. They were gossipy and malicious, noisy and quarrelsome. The children were addicted to the appropriation of the property of others—which is a gentle way of saying that they were a pack of junior-sized thieves. Collectively they were a thorn in the flesh of the neighborhood.

On our land but close to, and shading, their kitchen window was the most miserable skeleton of a peach tree that anyone ever saw. Every spring the gnarled old tree would, with great effort, gather together all of its little store of strength and produce a few leaves, a few blossoms. In due season the blossoms would develop into tiny, hard green peaches that never matured. They were good for only one thing—throwing. You can guess who threw them and where. It had always been so; the tree was so completely unproductive that Mother decided to have it cut down and to put flowers in its place.

It wasn't long before word of her decision reached the neighbors. They rushed over to plead with her to permit the old tree to stand because it was the only shade that they had on their kitchen. Their kitchen had a flat roof, and it was exposed to the merciless Illinois sun. It was a tempting picture, those rascals sweltering in their doubly-heated kitchen. There was certainly poetic justice in it; they had turned the heat on us often enough, and one could easily be tempted to see a prophetic element in the situation. But Mother was a Christian and believed that she ought to act like one. She said, "Of course I will leave the tree," and she did.

When spring came that year something wonderful had happened to the tree. Those bony old limbs disappeared into a great cloud of blossoms. The blossoms developed into the tiny, hard green peaches that we had known across the years, and then, wonder of wonder, they matured and became wonderful, sweet, delicious fruit.

We ate all that we could; Mother gave some away to the neighbors, including the unpleasant ones, and she canned enough to last us all through the coming year.

In a few months the neighbors moved. I do not mean to suggest that there is any connection here. But they did move; I am only

reporting the facts. And that year, or the next, the tree died.

The tree had never produced good fruit before; it never produced good fruit again: it did so just that one year. I know what some of you are thinking—the tree would have produced fruit even if Mother had not been so nice; it was something about the season or the chemicals. I don't know why it happened; I do not claim to. But I do know this: if she had returned evil for evil, it would not have happened for there would have been no tree, and a small ~~boy~~ girl would have missed one of the most beautiful experiences and one of the deepest lessons of ~~his~~ her whole life.

Mother had an opportunity to get even and instead, she sowed love, and there came forth a wonderful harvest. There was a harvest on the tree but there was also a harvest in her soul, in mine, in many others.

A D A P T E D   F R O M   A   S P E E C H   B Y   P A S T O R   D O N A L D   E W I N G .

THE SHEPHERD'S PSALM
Robert Strand

FROM *ESPECIALLY FOR THE HURTING HEART*

There is a story of an old man and a young man on the same platform before an audience. A special part of the program was being presented. Each of the men was to repeat from memory the Twenty-third Psalm. The young man, trained in speech and drama, gave in oratory, the Psalm. When finished the audience clapped for more so that they could hear his beautiful, modulated voice once more.

Then the old man, leaning on his cane, stepped to the front of the platform and in a feeble, shaking voice, repeated the same words. But when he was seated no sound came from the listeners.

Folks wiped tears as they seemed to pray. In the ensuing silence, the young man again stepped forward and made the following statement: "Friends, I wish to make an explanation. You asked me to repeat the Psalm with your applause, but you remained silent when my friend was finished. The difference? I shall tell you. I know the Psalm, but he knows the Shepherd of the Psalm."

THE LORD IS MY SHEPHERD

The LORD is my shepherd; I shall not want.

He maketh me to lie down in green pastures;

He leadeth me beside the still waters.

He restoreth my soul:

He leadeth me in the paths of righteousness for his name's sake.

Yea, though I walk through the valley of the shadow of death,

I will fear no evil: for thou art with me;

Thy rod and thy staff they comfort me.

Thou preparest a table before me in the presence of mine enemies:

Thou anointest my head with oil; my cup runneth over.

Surely goodness and mercy shall follow me all the days of my life:

And I will dwell in the house of the LORD forever.

PSALM 23

MARGARET AND HER PENNIES
Philip Gulley

FROM *HOME TOWN TALES*

very Monday morning, my friend Jim and I eat breakfast at Bob Evans' and swap war stories. Jim pastors an inner-city church, and his stories have more meat and gristle than mine.

One morning he told me about Margaret. Margaret is an eighty-year-old widow in his church. She lives in a retirement center and ventures out once a week to buy groceries at Safeway. Margaret, Jim reports, is a sweet lady, though that hasn't always been the case. She told Jim that when she was younger she was not a good person, but God has slowly changed her. Occasionally, God builds the house overnight, but most times God nails up one board each day. Margaret was a board each day.

Several years ago, Margaret felt God wanted her to do something for her inner-city church. So she prayed about it, and after a while the Lord told her to save all her pennies for the children of the church. Margaret was hoping for something a little grander, but she didn't complain. A person has to start somewhere, she told Jim. So every year at Christmas, she wrapped up her pennies, about ten

dollars' worth, and gave them to her church. She told them it was for the kids and not to spend it on pew cushions.

One afternoon a lady down the hall from Margaret came to visit. She noticed Margaret's mayonnaise jar full of pennies. She asked her why she was saving pennies. Margaret told her it was for the kids at church.

"I don't have a church," the lady said. "Can I save up my pennies and give them to the kids in your church?"

"Suit yourself," Margaret said.

Before long, thirty folks in the retirement center were saving their pennies for the kids.

Every Wednesday, they climb on the retirement center's bus and drive to the Safeway. They steer their carts up and down the aisles, then stand in line at the checkout counter. They put their groceries on the moving belt and watch as each price pops up on the display. When the checker calls the total, the old folks count out the money a bill at a time. Then they ask for the change in pennies. They count that out, too, one penny at a time. The other customers stand behind them and roll their eyes. They don't know a work of God is underway.

The next year at Christmastime, the women loaded up their jars and took their pennies, twenty thousand of them, to the church

Christmas party. The kids staggered from the Christmas party, their pockets bursting with pennies.

When the kids found out who was behind the pennies, they wanted to visit the retirement center and sing Christmas carols. Pastor Jim took them in Big Blue, the church bus. They assembled in the dining room. Jim watched from the back row. In front of him sat one of the retirement center ladies. Jim didn't know her, had never seen her. She was explaining to a visitor what was going on.

"These children, you see, they're from our church, and they've come to visit us. We're awfully close."

The next week, one of the men in the retirement center passed away. Jim came and conducted the memorial service right there at the retirement center, which is fast becoming the new church annex.

All of this, mind you, began with Margaret in her apartment praying to the Lord to let her do a mighty work. She admits now that she was a little disappointed when God told her to save her pennies. She was hoping for a more flamboyant ministry. She didn't want to start with pennies. Then she thought back on her own life and how sometimes God builds houses one board each day.

UNANSWERED LETTERS

Author unknown

I read of a man who was involved in a tragic accident. He lost both legs and his left arm and only a finger and thumb remained on the right hand. But he still possessed a brilliant mind, enriched with a good education and broadened with world travel. At first he thought there was nothing he could do but remain a helpless sufferer.

A thought came to him. It was always nice to receive letters, but why not write them—he could still use his right hand with some difficulty. But to whom could he write?

Was there anyone shut in and incapacitated like he was who could be encouraged by his letters? He thought of men in prison—they did have some hope of release whereas he had none—but it was worth a try.

He wrote to a Christian organization concerned with prison ministry. He was told that his letters could not be answered—it was against prison rules, but he commenced this one-sided correspondence.

He wrote twice a week, and it taxed his strength to the limit. But into the letters he put his whole soul, all his experience, all his faith, all his wit, and all his Christian optimism. Frequently he felt discouraged and was tempted to give it up. But it was his one remaining activity, and he resolved to continue as long as he could.

At last he got a letter. It was very short, written on prison stationery by the officer whose duty it was to censor the mail. All it said was: "Please write on the best paper you can afford. Your letters are passed from cell to cell till they literally fall to pieces."

No matter what our personal situation is, we still have God-given gifts and talents, experiences, and encouragement that we can share with others.

As a spring bubbles forth refreshment
So does a cheerful thought.
—*Kimber Annie Engstrom*

V E R N A ' S   S E C R E T

Linda Andersen

F R O M   *S L I C E S   O F   L I F E*

*S*he lives alone in tiny, second-story rooms above a weather-beaten general store and gas station that have seen better days. No one has used them for years. Verna Bok has been a widow for 40 years, I learned one Sunday after church. This diminutive lady without a car is always in church (when she's well), and she's always smiling. I wondered why as I watched her come and go, leaning heavily on her cane.

The blinds at Verna's windows are slightly askew and the building she lives in looks perpetually deserted and forgotten. A lone gas pump sits stolidly out in front near the road like a paunch, middle-aged man with nothing much to do except watch the traffic go by. The old, sun-faded pump hasn't served our lazy little community in more years than anyone can remember. The cost of gasoline still reads 31 cents a gallon—just as if inflation never happened—just as if it remembers a time when our tiny farming town boasted enough "live" businesses to keep the main road buzzing with activity. Verna remembers those days well enough. Now business has

gone elsewhere, leaving the village of Forest Grove and Verna to grow old together. But Verna Bok is not a person who merely sits still and grows old, as I soon discovered.

I was having some neighbors in one evening, and on a sudden impulse I decided to include Verna.

"How nice!" she beamed over the telephone wire connecting our voices. "How very nice of you to call. I'd surely come if I was well enough." She had been sick for a couple of weeks up there alone in that tiny apartment. I was sorry, and I told her so.

"You must get awfully lonesome, Verna."

"Lonesome?" She sounded surprised. "Oh my, no," she bubbled, laughing. "Why, I'm never lonesome." (I had a feeling I was about to discover something.) "You see, I have all my good memories to keep me company—and my photograph albums too. And then, o' course, I keep so busy with Ruth's boys."

"Oh?" I asked, before remembering that she had a nearby neighbor named Ruth.

"Oh yes," she replied. "You see, Ruth has raised them eight boys by herself ever since the divorce, and she works, ya know. So's I fix supper for them boys every night. Yes, I been doin' it for years. It saves her a whole lot of worry and it gives me sumthin' useful to

do. Oh, yes, them boys gets me flowers too, on Mother's Day. They're like m'own boys." Now I knew that this was an unusual person indeed. And I began to understand the secret of her youthful exuberance for life.

Verna had learned something that most people take a lifetime to discover, and she had found it less than a country mile from her own home. Without actually looking for happiness, she had kept herself busy filling the empty cups of other people's lives.

When my husband greeted Verna in church one morning some weeks later, he commented on the stunning pair of cardinals he had spotted in our maple trees. "Verna," he emphasized, "they would have knocked your eyes out!" Her warm eyes brightened, and her familiar smile appeared.

"Oh yes," she chuckled. "And you know, I heard the most beautiful wren song just this morning." She shook her finger for emphasis as she talked. "I get up early every day, ya know, so's I don't miss a thing. I like to watch the houses around here wake up, don'tcha know. Yessir, there's so much ta see—so much ta see. And I enjoy everything God has made—everything, don'tcha see?" The secret was finally out.

Verna, you get up to see what most of us miss, or ignore, or are

just too busy to enjoy. You magnify the plusses God places all over your small world. You seem to paint a rainbow around every little event, even the early morning song of a little bird. There's no need to feel sorry for you, Verna. None whatever. You have no time to feel sorry for yourself. You're too busy giving thanks and enjoying things.

Keep it up, Verna. Your sunshiny ways are bringing God's light to a lot of lives—including mine.

*Do not have your concert first and
tune your instrument afterward.
Begin each day with God.*
—James Taylor Hudson

JUST BECAUSE I LOVE YOU
Suzanne F. Diaz
FROM *VIRTUE* MAGAZINE

On a beautiful spring day, I took my lunch break outside on a bench under a huge, shady tree. I was alone, but it was nice to leave my workplace and spend some time outside, having a little picnic of one.

Lately I'd been reflecting on the loneliness in my life, several years after a divorce and a major move. I'd finished raising my family alone and was occupied with surviving in the '90s working world. Perhaps that was why I had not met a new mate, someone with whom I could share my life and my love. I'd not really ever entered the arena of singles, which was always dominated by a greater number of women (and young women, at that) than men. I kept very busy with my teenage daughter's activities and visiting my grown children and my new grandson, as well as being involved with my church groups.

At the office there were quite a few married women, who sometimes received flowers at work from their husbands. The arrangements often had notes attached, telling them the flowers were sent

"just because I love you." I admired the flowers, but, even more, the sentiments behind them. Unhappily married for many years, I had never become accustomed to receiving anything just because I was loved. I longed for flowers like those and envied those loved women.

At the picnic table, as I started my meal, I felt something fall on my head. It was a blossom on its way down to the grass. I looked up and saw that the huge tree I was sitting under was full of graceful magenta flowers, which hung within fairly easy reach. I hadn't even noticed them, because I hadn't looked up.

I immediately saw that I was being gifted with flowers, beautiful flowers from Someone who loved me. God wasn't going to leave me without my own token of His love! I stood on a low brick ledge and gathered a few low-hanging blossoms. I took them back to my desk, and placed them in a glass jar. It was wonderful to see them as I worked, and to be reminded during the day that God wanted me to have flowers, just because He loved me.

PERSPECTIVE

A little girl was visiting her grandmother in the country. One evening they sat and enjoyed the panorama of stars in the heavens—such sparkling brilliance the little girl hadn't seen, living in the city with all the lights. She was in awe of the beauty and said to her grandmother, "If heaven is so beautiful on the wrong side, what must it be like on the right side?"

Marilyn McAuley

FROM *MORE STORIES FOR THE HEART*

GUEST OF THE MAESTRO
Max Lucado

FROM WHEN GOD WHISPERS YOUR NAME

What happens when a dog interrupts a concert? To answer that, come with me to a spring night in Lawrence, Kansas. Take your seat in Hoch Auditorium and behold the Leipzig Gewandhaus Orchestra—the oldest continually operating orchestra in the world. The greatest composers and conductors in history have directed this orchestra. It was playing in the days of Beethoven (some of the musicians have been replaced).

You watch as stately dressed Europeans take their seats on the stage. You listen as professionals carefully tune their instruments. The percussionist puts her ear to the kettle drum. A violinist plucks the nylon string. A clarinet player tightens the reed. And you sit a bit straighter as the lights dim and the tuning stops. The music is about to begin.

The conductor, dressed in tails, strides onto the stage, springs onto the podium, and gestures for the orchestra to rise. You and two thousand others applaud. The musicians take their seats, the maes-

tro takes his position, and the audience holds its breath.

There is a second of silence between lightning and thunder. And there is a second of silence between the raising of the baton and the explosion of the music. But when it falls the heavens open and you are delightfully drenched in the downpour of Beethoven's Third Symphony.

Such was the power of that spring night in Lawrence, Kansas. That hot, spring night in Lawrence, Kansas. I mention the temperature so you'll understand why the doors were open. It was hot. Hoch Auditorium, a historic building, was not air-conditioned. Combine bright stage lights with formal dress and furious music, and the result is a heated orchestra. Outside doors on each side of the stage were left open in case of a breeze.

Enter, stage right, the dog. A brown, generic, Kansas dog. Not a mean dog. Not a mad dog. Just a curious dog. He passes between the double basses and makes his way through the second violins and into the cellos. His tail wags in beat with the music. As the dog passes between the players, they look at him, look at each other, and continue with the next measure.

The dog takes a liking to a certain cello. Perhaps it was the lateral passing of the bow. Maybe it was the eye-level view of the

strings. Whatever it was, it caught the dog's attention and he stopped and watched. The cellist wasn't sure what to do. He'd never played for a canine audience. And music schools don't teach you what dog slobber might do to the lacquer of a sixteenth-century Guarneri cello. But the dog did nothing but watch for a moment and then move on.

Had he passed on through the orchestra, the music might have continued. Had he made his way across the stage into the motioning hands of a stagehand, the audience might never have noticed. But he didn't leave. He stayed. At home in the splendor. Roaming through the meadows of music.

He visited the woodwinds, turned his head at the trumpets, stepped between the flutists, and stopped by the side of the conductor. And Beethoven's Third Symphony came undone.

The musicians laughed. The audience laughed. The dog looked up at the conductor and panted. And the conductor lowered his baton.

The most historic orchestra in the world. One of the most moving pieces ever written. A night wrapped in glory, all brought to a stop by a wayward dog.

The chuckles ceased as the conductor turned. What fury might erupt? The audience grew quiet as the maestro faced them. What

fuse had been lit? The polished, German director looked at the crowd, looked down at the dog, then looked back at the people, raised his hands in a universal gesture and...shrugged.

Everyone roared.

He stepped off the podium and scratched the dog behind the ears. The tail wagged again. The maestro spoke to the dog. He spoke in German, but the dog seemed to understand. The two visited for a few seconds before the maestro took his new friend by the collar and led him off the stage. You'd have thought the dog was Pavarotti the way the people applauded. The conductor returned and the music began and Beethoven seemed none the worse for the whole experience.

Can you find you and me in this picture?

I can. Just call us Fido. And consider God the Maestro.

And envision the moment when we will walk onto his stage. We won't deserve to. We will not have earned it. We may even surprise the musicians with our presence.

The music will be like none we've ever heard. We'll stroll among the angels and listen as they sing. We'll gaze at heaven's lights and gasp as they shine. And we'll walk next to the Maestro, stand by his side, and worship as he leads.... See the unseen and live for that

event. We are invited to tune our ears to the song of the skies and long—long for the moment when we'll be at the Maestro's side.

He, too, will welcome. And he, too, will speak. But he will not lead us away. He will invite us to remain, forever his guests on his stage.

*A smile of encouragement at the right moment
may act like sunlight on a closed-up flower;
it may be the turning point for a struggling life.*
—*Author unknown*

PEACE

The sea was beating against the rocks in huge, dashing waves. The lightning was flashing, the thunder was roaring, the wind was blowing; but the little bird was asleep in the crevice of the rock, its head serenely under its wing, sound asleep.

That is peace—to be able to sleep in the storm! In Christ, we are relaxed and at peace in the midst of the confusions, bewilderments, and perplexities of this life. The storm rages, but our hearts are at rest. We have found peace—at last!

Billy Graham
FROM *UNTO THE HILLS*

ACKNOWLEDGMENTS

A diligent search has been made to trace original ownership, and when necessary, permission to reprint has been obtained. If I have overlooked giving proper credit to anyone, please accept my apologies. Should any attribution be found to be incorrect, the publisher welcomes written documentation supporting correction for subsequent printings. For material not in the public domain, grateful acknowledgment is given to the publishers and individuals who have granted permission for use of their material.

Acknowledgments are listed by story title in the order they appear in the book. For permission to reprint any of the stories please request permission from the original source listed below.

SUNNY MOMENTS

Quotes by Kimber Annie Engstrom © 2000. Used by permission of the author. E-mail: kengstrom@coinet.com.

"Love and the Cabbie" by Art Buchwald. © 1993. Used by permission of the author.

"Lesson in Forgiveness" by Jerry Harpt. © 1997. A retired teacher/counselor, Jerry writes young adult books and freelances with travel columns and human interest stories. Used by permission of the author.

"Summer Vacation" by Bruce Larson. Taken from *The One and Only You* by Bruce Larson, © 1974, Word Publishing, Nashville, Tennessee. All rights reserved. Used by permission.

"A Mother's Love" by David Giannelli. David is a fireman for Ladder Company 175, 165 Bradford Street, Brooklyn, New York 11207. This story first appeared in *Chicken Soup for the Pet Lover's Soul*. Used by permission of the author.

"The Dance" by Thelda Bevens, quoted from *A Passage through Grief* by Barbara Baumgardner (Broadman and Holman Publishers, Nashville, TN, © 1997). Used by permission of Thelda Bevens.

WHIMSICAL DAYS

"Lookin' Good" by Patsy Clairmont. Taken from *God Uses Cracked Pots* by Patsy Clairmont, a Focus on the Family book published by Tyndale House. Copyright © 1991. All rights reserved. International copyright secured. Used by permission.

"New Friends" by Teri Leinbaugh, freelance writer, Richland, MO. Quoted from *The Christian Reader*, May/June 1992. Used by permission of the author.

"Grandma's Laughter" by Casandra Lindell, freelance editor and writer under the company name *The Write Word*, Portland, OR. Previously published in *Stories for a Family's Heart*. © 1998. Used by permission of the author.

"Molly" by Barbara Baumgardner. © 1999. Barbara shares a home in Oregon with her golden retriever, Molly. Used by permission of the author.

"Longer, Daddy... Longer!" by Gary Smalley and John Trent. Taken from *Leaving the Light On* by Gary Smalley and John Trent. © 1994. Used by permission of Multnomah Publishers, Inc.

"The Gift of Gab" by Lynn Rogers Petrak. © 1996. This story was originally published in *Chicken Soup for the Woman's Soul*. Used by permission of the author.

"Lifted" by Rochelle M. Pennington, freelance writer, newspaper columnist, and contributing author to *Stories for the Heart, Chicken Soup for the Soul*, and *Life's Little Instruction Book*. You may contact her at N1911 Double D Rd., Campbellsport, WI 53010, (920) 533-5880. Used by permission of the author.

"Valentines" by Dale Galloway. Taken from *Dream a New Dream* (Tyndale House Publishers, © 1975). Used by permission of the author.

"The Student's Mite" by David R. Collins, freelance writer, Moline, IL. Quoted from *Teachers in Focus* magazine, December 1996/January 1997. Used by permission of the author.

"I Love You Anyway" by Dr. Joe A. Harding, author of *Growth*

Plus and coauthor of *Vision 2000*. Joe Harding calls the church to turn from negative images to positive Biblical images of hope. He is widely known as a dynamic speaker and leader. Previously published in *Stories for a Kindred Heart*. © 1999. Used by permission of the author.

Home Town Tales by Philip Gulley. © 1998. Used by permission of Multnomah Publishers, Inc.

"Verna's Secret" by Linda Andersen. Taken from *Slices of Life* (Baker Book House © 1986). Used by permission of the author. Linda Andersen is the author of four inspirational books for women and is published 500 times in 35 publications. *Love Adds the Chocolate* (Waterbrook Press) will be rereleased summer 2000.

"Just Because I Love You" by Suzanne F. Diaz, freelance writer, Claremont, CA. As printed in *Virtue* magazine, June/July 1998. Used by permission of the author.

"Perspective" by Marilyn McAuley. Previously published in *More Stories for the Heart*, © 1997. Used by permission of the author.

"Guest of the Maestro" by Max Lucado. Taken from *When God Whispers Your Name* by Max Lucado, © 1994, Word Publishing, Nashville, Tennessee. All rights reserved. Used by permission.

"Peace" by Billy Graham. Taken from *Unto the Hills* by Billy Graham, © 1996, Word Publishing, Nashville, Tennessee. All rights reserved. Used by permission.